For my darling
Tydusseus
~N.E.

For Marcus, who
makes me happy
~K.H.

Text copyright © 2018 by Caterpillar Books
Jacket art and interior illustrations copyright © 2018 by Katie Hickey
Text written by Nicola Edwards

Visit us on the Web! rhcbooks.com

Educators and librarians, for a variety of teaching tools, visit us at RHTeachersLibrarians.com

Library of Congress Cataloging-in-Publication Data is available upon request.
ISBN 978-0-593-12119-1 (trade) — ISBN 978-0-593-12120-7 (ebook)
CPB/1800/1311/1119

MANUFACTURED IN CHINA
10 9 8 7 6 5 4 3 2 1
First American Edition

happy

By **Nicola Edwards**

Illustrated by **Katie Hickey**

Rodale Kids New York

Mindfulness

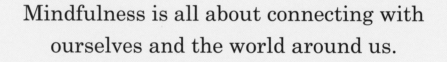

Mindfulness is all about connecting with
ourselves and the world around us.

Let's take a journey together to discover
some simple steps on the path to happiness.

Real life is right under our noses.

We can miss it by rushing around.

But stopping to smell life's sweet roses

is where **true**

happiness

can be found.

Listening

When we're still,

there is space then to listen

to the sweet song of wind in the trees,

the gruff rumble of cars in the distance,

or the whisper of

rustling leaves.

Take a moment to stop and really listen
to the sounds around you.

Feeling

Even the darkest storm passes.

The sun can't shine bright every day.

We can sit with our feelings and notice

how they roll through us,

then blow away.

What kinds of things
make you feel happy?

Relaxing

It's not just our **minds** we get trapped in.

Our bodies can feel **tension** too.

We can **loosen** our limbs when that happens.

Like the **sun** from the **clouds**,

we **break through**.

Try tensing up all of your muscles

and then relaxing them, one by one.

Tasting

Whether hot, salty, sweet, or sour flavor,

we taste and we chew and we feel.

If we slow when we eat, we can savor

the deliciousness of every meal.

Do you notice different textures and flavors
when you chew your food slowly?

Touching

Touch calms the **wildest emotions**.

We **connect** to the world all around

when we dip our toes into the ocean
or crunch crisp golden leaves on the ground.

Close your eyes, and see if you can tell
what things are just by touching them.

Discovering

Exploring is one of life's pleasures.

Spot a penny, a shell, or a brook.

The world's brimming with

curious treasures

for the people who

take time to look.

Look all around you,

and try to spot something

you haven't noticed before.

Smelling

When we're all tangled up in our worries,

the cool air gets us grounded again—

woodsmoke through the sharp tang of pine trees

or the freshness of earth after rain.

Do the things you can smell make you feel
anything or bring back any memories?

Loving

The warmth of a hug can work wonders.

Being happy is something you feed

with a smile or a touch or a kindness.

Even the tallest tree grows from a seed.

Have you given someone
a smile or a hug today?

Appreciating

It feels good to give thanks at the day's end

for the pink blushing sky overhead,

a hot meal, comfy shoes, or a good friend,

and the warmth of a soft cozy bed.

What good things have happened in your world today?

Breathing

We breathe deep and expand like the galaxy.

We breathe out many thousands of stars.

And if ever we start to feel panicky,

this reminds us of just who we are.

Take a deep breath, hold it for two seconds,

and then breathe out very slowly.

Happiness

Real life is right under our noses.

It's what's here, not the **future** or **past**.

Every day is a fresh new adventure.

Now we live in the moment, at last.

How can you be more mindful each and every day?